EMOTION LOTION

the simple guide to
Mental Hygiene
and retaining your sanity

Fiona Ross

Dear Liz
Peace and Plenty

Fiona

Published in Great Britain in 2017
Under the **HypnoArts** label by
the Academy of Hypnotic Arts Ltd.
1 Emperor Way, Exeter, EX13QS

Hypnoarts.com

Enquiries should be addressed to the
Academy of Hypnotic Arts.
bookpub@hypnoarts.com

First printed edition 2017
British Library Cataloguing in Publication Data
ISBN Number: 978-1-9997641-7-3

This book is dedicated;

To the people I have known and to those I have not, who's lives have given my life meaning and purpose.

To the people who have inspired me and to those who have challenged me.

To the love, the tears and the Joy.

To the smiles from strangers, and most of all to the adversity - for that is where I have learned the most.

Always grateful,

Fiona

CONTENTS

Forward
by Penny Power OBE

If you have a strong mind, you will build a strong business, this has been the belief system I have held for over 20 years and I am delighted to read the book written by Fiona Ross that shines a light on the need for Mental Hygiene. The need to keep our minds clear so that we can manage the turbulence of owning a business and ensure we are alert, resilient, positive and in control of our daily activities and mindset, will have a significant impact on the longevity and success of your business.

Sector knowledge, listening to the market, connecting and building your brand, all these skills, and many more, will help you achieve your goals. Increasingly the business world is becoming more transparent with the rise in social communications. Anxiety, stress and depression knock at the door of too many business owners. We all have to invest in our mental strength as much as we invest in our practical and intellectual knowledge.

There are many books on personal development, the sales of books are growing in line with the awareness that this subject is critical and we have to take ownership of our mental state.

Fiona brings her experiences, gained through travel, research and personal needs in a conversational and light way. You will feel she is sitting next to you, holding your hand and your heart.

Enjoy, make the most of your precious life and maintain your mental hygiene on a daily basis to bring peace and calm, enabling you to have the life you want.

A note on how this book was created

This book was originally created as a live interview. That's why it reads as a conversation rather than a traditional book that talks 'at you'. It's also why it isn't after an award for literature, but it will engage, educate and empower you.

I wanted you to feel as though I am talking 'with you', much like a close friend or relative. I felt that creating the material this way would make it easier for you to grasp the topics and put them to use quickly, rather than wading through hundreds of heavily edited pages.

So relax, and get ready to get a better work life balance, enjoy more free time and live every day of your life.

Let's get started and apply Emotion Lotion daily...

Fiona Ross

Introduction

Hi everyone and welcome to: Emotion Lotion the simple guide to Mental Hygiene and retaining your sanity...

This is Jonathan Chase for HypnoArts and today I'm talking with author, and international speaker, Fiona Ross.

This book is for everyone but, especially for solopreneur's because running your own business is as stressful as moving house or getting married, and generally lasts longer.

This is an easy to read, and easier to apply, eclectic guide to retaining your sanity with mental hygiene.

Fiona Ross is a former educator for L'Oreal, now Expert Mind Coach, Advanced Hypnotist and NLP Master practitioner with over 18 years experience living India and South East Asia practicing Vipassana Meditation. In India she ran and owned her own business and was privileged to have received a blessing from His Holiness the

14th Dalai Lama at his home in the Himalayas.

Fiona has been running her successful, Surrey-based, subconscious Mind Coaching Business for the last 7 years.

In this book, conducted as an interview to maintain the real voice of the author, and to make you feel as if you are really part of the conversation. Fiona shows you how a simple and straightforward daily application of this practical psychology, that she calls Emotion Lotion, helps you to think clearly and feel better.

What is Emotion Lotion?

Jon: So, Fiona, in a short sentence or two, what is Emotion Lotion?

Fiona: Well, Jon, Emotion Lotion is an approach that I've developed using mental hygiene. It's a type of practical psychology that you can apply daily, so that solopreneurs and business owners like you and I, can retain our sanity, get a better work-life balance, enjoy more time, and live every day of our lives.

Fiona's Story:

Jon: Tell us, Fiona, how did you get here?

Fiona: Okay, well I would just like to set the
         scene a little bit there for you Jon,
         because I started my career as a very
         enthusiastic apprentice in the hair and
         beauty industry, "which," I worked
         very hard at.

         I became training manager at Harrods
         and I've worked for Toni & Guy, my
         career then went into working for
         L'Oréal as an educator and trainer.

         I decided to leave all of that and go
         travelling for six months.

         I went off to India and I loved it so
         much, 18 years later, after a lot of
         adventures and a lot of wonderful

things happened to me, I returned to the UK after the universe decided to play Kerplunk with me.

You probably know the game Kerplunk where you have all the little straws that are pulled out and it all just collapses on you.

Well, that's kind of what happened.

Various things in my life fell apart, my marriage, my visa situation in India and where I was living became untenable. So many things started to go wrong and I had to wrap up there in 2010 and start again, just boot strap and start again.

That's exactly where I came to and I started my Mind Coaching business.

As you know, starting a business is probably one of the most difficult things you can do and you probably start it from a very naïve position of thinking you're just going to get to

do what you are trained to do.
And what you don't realise is that
you've got to be all the other things
that a business has, like the
accountant, and the marketing person,
and you have to get the internet
working and all sorts of other things.

That is a really stressful process.
There's a lot of us out there trying
very hard to build successful
businesses and we're living in quite a
mad world. Our sanity is stretched
every single day.

So Emotion Lotion, really, are the
methods I used to get myself to the
point I'm at now running a successful
business, enjoying the process and
living every day of my life.

Jon: You are now a full-time mind coach.
          Is Emotion Lotion the approach that
          you've developed so that you use it all
          the time?

Fiona: Yes, this is how I live *my* life.

These are the presets I use in my world, learned over many years.

A lot of it I learned in India from the holy men and the gurus and the meditations and all of those things that I experienced out there.

But applying it to a modern-day western lifestyle has enabled me to just enjoy my life and not get bogged down in the stresses and strains and all the crazy stuff that we see on television every day.

Jon: I've got to ask you about this, but you've got to tell us about the holy man in India story.

Fiona: Yes...

I've met a lot of holy men but there was one particular incident where we were invited to go to a temple where this holy man lived.

He was ashen covered and had dreadlocks. He was sitting in his room with a Trishula, which is a three pronged ritual weapon, like a trident, I suppose would be our equivalent.

From that was hanging a skull.

He cooked us a lovely meal but this particular type of Sadhu, or holy man, was an Aghori and part of their initiation is that they have to eat human flesh.

So, yes, I *was* cooked a meal by a cannibalistic holy man. It was probably one of the most interesting things I've ever done.

Jon: Was there any meat in the meal?

Fiona: There was, thankfully, *no* meat involved.

         It was a vegetarian meal, thank you!

Jon: So where are your focuses now?

Fiona: My focus is actually on living a really
         enjoyable life as a whole rather than
         having my life divided up into work
         and home and fun.

         It all runs very smoothly as one
         continuous thing. Helping others do
         the same has become my work,
         which is going very well.

         I have a successful business and an
         office in Weybridge, Surrey where I
         see my clients.

         My focus is now to move my
         coaching business forward to
         incorporate more business people,
         more entrepreneurs and help them
         get their businesses to where they
         want them to be, without all the
         stress and strain behind it, so they
         can sleep at night.

Jon: Fiona, what's going on in the world
         right now that makes solopreneurs

need your practical psychology techniques in mental hygiene more than ever?

Fiona: Every day I have people come to see me in my office and they're essentially suffering from poor mental hygiene.

They don't know how to think or they're believing the things that they think are really them.

This leads them to suffer from sleep problems, stress, anxiety, depression, all sorts of issues that essentially cause them to become stuck and unable to move on in their lives. They just get stuck at that point where they just don't know what to do next.

They don't know how to get themselves out of the situations that they're in and they find themselves in a downward spiral where they're really just not functioning properly in one or all of the areas of their lives.

With all the bad news that we watch on television, with social media, with all the modern-day world that we live in, people are taking all of that on and they're just not able to think their way through it.

They're not able to actually get themselves to a point where they can let go of all that stuff and actually enjoy the day, enjoy the moment and enjoy this beautiful world that we live in.

Jon: And how does that equate particularly for solopreneurs?

Fiona: Well, unless you're functioning as your true authentic self, you're not going to be able to run that through your business. You're not going to have a congruent message that goes out to your clients.

We know people buy people, and so

the person behind a solopreneur business is vital to the message that they give out.

So, unless you're a happy, engaged human being that is confident in what you're doing, you're going to find your business is going to struggle because people aren't going to see the authenticity in what you do. And they're not going to get that congruent message all the way through your business.

What's Going On?

Jon: Is the zeitgeist in a place where this is going to be staying pretty much the same?

Fiona: It's possibly going to get worse.

The more we buy into media, the more we buy into the craziness that we have no control over in the world, the more unhappy we become. People aren't really looking at their own world and seeing what they do have control over and making their world happy.

There's a lovely phrase that I learned in India that was, "If we swept outside our own door, the whole world would be clean."

It really applies that principle, if you sort out your own thinking and you sort out your own mind, then everything else becomes less of a problem.

I think we're entering a huge period of change and I think we're going to find that laws will also be changing.

Many small businesses are going to find that the way that they've been operating in the past is going to be different, so we've got the keep abreast of those changes.

That can be quite scary for some people.

We need to be operating from a point of calm so when those changes come, we can just accept them and roll with them, if you like. Rather than them becoming an obstacle that could actually cost us our livelihoods.

Mental Hygiene And Its Impact On Our Emotions

Jon: So Fiona, what's the impact, the result of the practical psychology of Mental Hygiene on people's emotions?

Fiona: Well, there are two main areas here Jon.

One being mental health.

Mental health is something that's in the news a lot at the moment.

We see mental health issues are on the increase and there's a lot of people doing some really good work in that field to help all sorts of people with these issues.

However, there is a large majority of people that feel that they have something wrong in their thinking and really all they're suffering from is poor mental hygiene.

It's the learning how to think, it's learning how to control your thoughts and be at peace with what goes on in your mind that brings about the changes in your everyday life.

You don't have to have a mental health issue when you have a problem.

The second thing is we are bombarded by news all the time.

A lot of this news we have absolutely no control over.

The news feed tends to be a repetitive over and over and over thing. When people get caught up in that, it affects their thinking.

They'll be thinking about it all day.

They could lose sleep over issues they have absolutely no control over and that has a huge impact on their lives.

And really, just remembering that not every issue is a problem and not every issue needs to be a big important thing in life.

I think we're not taught about this.

We need to have this education actually starting at a very young age.

It's great to see things like mindfulness being taught in schools and more practical ways of controlling the mind.

Because it's in our mind.

Everything is in our mind, it's where it all starts.

It all starts with the way we think and if we learn poor habits when we're young, they often escalate into much bigger habits when we're older.

There are many things out there that people can do to help themselves with this issue.

The first thing is *identifying* that we need to change the way we think.

We need to change the way we view the world and the way we relate to the world around us.

Jon: So what can we do about it?

Fiona: We can apply some very simple techniques to our lives.

We can learn some very simple things to just make that a lot easier and we'll be going into that a little bit later in more detail.

Jon: Okay, and that's what you call Emotion Lotion?

Fiona: That is Emotion Lotion.
It's techniques you can apply every day to take the pressure off, to lower

the tension in life.

So you really can get on and enjoy what you do and enjoy your family, enjoy your friends.

And as I said, enjoy this beautiful world that we live in.

What Are The Alternatives?

Jon: So Fiona, we know solopreneurs stress is never going to go away, but what currently is being done? What are the alternatives we need to be aware of?

Fiona: There are many alternatives out there and there are many self-help books on the shelves.

One of the things that people like to do is meditate but learning an effective meditation technique can take weeks.

I have done several of these long, lengthy meditations.

First time I went to a beautiful centre up in the Himalayas and I, probably quite naively, had signed myself up for a 10 day meditation retreat... That 10 day meditation retreat was one of the hardest things I have ever done in my life.

And, it was one of the most rewarding things I've ever done in my life!

I'm very happy that I did it and I actually plan to do some more.

But it was 10 days of sitting for 13 hours a day, learning a meditation technique.

Quite frankly, most solopreneurs just don't have the time and doing a diluted form of meditation isn't really going to cut the mustard. You're not really going to get the results that you want.

A lot of people meditate and they don't really know what they're doing.

They're just sitting there and their mind is still ruminating.

Their mind is still going over and over and over the problems that they're experiencing.

That's not really meditation.

The second thing that is banded about an awful lot is mindfulness.

And mindfulness is an incredibly powerful technique to use, but again it's become a bit of the 'it word' and there's an awful lot of very diluted mindfulness out there.

In fact the meditation technique that I learned all those years ago is the foundation of mindfulness.

The diluted forms that are coming out now have their use but they're not really effective unless you're applying them every single day.

So there are many things that people can do to help themselves and Emotion Lotion is really a potted version. It allows them to do simple things that they can apply every day and get that soothing feeling.

Jon: A lot of people, certainly like me, feel that we should meditate and that we should be more mindfully aware.

But, yes you're right, we just simply don't have the time.

So how do the modern meditation methods differ from what you learnt in India all those years ago?

Fiona: In the Vipassana meditation that I do, they talk of the monkey mind.

And the monkey mind is the mind that keeps running away and jumping around all through the trees and you have no control over the monkey mind.

The foundation of Vipassana is being able to bring that monkey mind back to the moment and sit with equanimity.

To not apply a positive or a negative to the situation and just really accept everything for what it is.

When you stop applying this positive and negative to everything that happens you find that suffering disappears.

There are many other types of meditations but very often you find that people that sit and meditate are just sitting with their monkey minds worrying about things that they have no control over.

Worrying about what they're going to eat for dinner tonight.

Worry about whether they've got time to pick up their children before they go to the netball class that their daughters got. To go up and then pick up all the other kids, and see some clients, and run their business.

So finding simple techniques, simple

things that you can apply every day and really catch yourself doing those negative mental thoughts, bringing them back to the moment, makes such a huge difference.

Jon: But still, presumably, you're still saying that a good meditation every now and again when you can.

Fiona: Absolutely, if you can find the time to do that.

But again, with solopreneurs, we're usually quite time poor so it's about finding that space in our lives.

We all have the great intentions of doing it, "Yes I'm going to meditate for half an hour every morning", but in reality that often doesn't happen.

So you really need to have techniques that you can use on the go throughout the day that actually become part of the way you live your life rather than something that you do separately.

What You Need To Do

Jon: So if Emotion Lotion's the answer, what do we, the people reading this, the people listening to it right now...

What's the right mindset or physical state we need to be in to get the most out of what's coming next?

Fiona: Ideally, I want you to get excited.

I just want you to be excited about getting a handle on your mindset.

A handle on your thinking, handle on your future and just knowing that it's actually a very enjoyable process to be on top of everything.

Jon: And what can the reader or listener be doing right now to say, get the most out of it?

Because people listen to this when they're doing exercise and stuff like that. Is there anything specific that you want the consumer of this to know?

Fiona: Well, it's interesting because a lot of people when they're struggling with their thoughts, find themselves in a space of fear, of anxiety or stress.

We can actually change that very rapidly into excitement because they run on the same nervous system.

Excitement and fear are just two sides of the same coin.

So if you can just flip that coin over and look at it as, "I'm excited. I'm ready to change, I'm ready to do what I need to do to start to really feel better," because that's what everybody wants to do, is to feel better.

Step 1. Acceptance - A Place To Start

Jon: Okay, Fiona so what's **step one** and how do we do it?

Fiona: *Acceptance is the place to start.*

Acceptance is one of our, if not the most, powerful of emotions that we can have.

When we learn to accept things as they are, only then can we actually have any control over them at all.

It's a little bit like if I was to pick up a ball and throw it at you, Jon. If you don't accept it by catching it, it's just going to hit you and it's going to hit you hard and it's going to hurt you.

Accepting things just the way they are gives you the power to make the changes to future things that are coming after you've accepted that one thing.

When I was a child, and I'm sure when you were a child, we were all told the "Row, Row, Row your boat," nursery rhyme.

[*Publishers note:*
The lyrics of the children's roundel nursery rhyme are...

"Row, row, row your boat,
Gently down the stream.
Merrily, merrily, merrily, merrily,
Life is but a dream!"]

Fiona: I loved this nursery rhyme because it explains to me exactly how we can live our lives happily.

It says, "Row, row, row **Your** boat."

Not anyone else's boat, **Your** boat...

And row it ***Gently down the stream***.
Not *up* the stream.

We want to go down the stream, and
we want to do it ***Merrily***!

And when we do it merrily, life is but a
dream.

I think that explains our lives and the
way to live them in such clarity that I
probably missed it when I was a child,
but it is a nursery rhyme that I love.

Because if we don't accept things as
they are and we don't accept things for
what they are, as Carl Jung said, "What
we resist, persists."

If we come up against something with
resistance we just keep bashing into
the same old stuff.

So just learning to accept things as
they are and as they are not is our

most powerful tool.

There's a little exercise that I like my clients to do and it has quite a profound effect on a person.

You can do it in the morning or in the evening.

We all use the bathroom first thing in the morning and most of us have a mirror in the bathroom.

This exercise involves you staring into the mirror and taking a good look at yourself and repeating the words out loud, "I love you for who you are and who you are not."

Accepting all parts of you as a person for the things that you are and the things that you're not.

By taking the pressure off yourself and taking an accepting view of who you are, an awful lot of that tension that you feel in life just melts away.

So you can stand in front of your mirror every morning, repeat this 10 times, or as many times as you feel that you want to actually, but 10 times would be a great place to start.

And see how you feel after you've done that, actually really accepting yourself for who you are and for who you are not.

Step 2. Don't Miss The Moment

Jon: Okay, step two. What's step two and
        how do we do it?

Fiona: **Step two is,** *Don't Miss the Moment.*

        We all live our lives rushing around
        and living in the past.

        So we're either running into the future
        or looking back at the past.

        I kind of see my life as a conveyor belt
        and it runs in one direction.

        My future lives off to this side and my
        past lives off down here and in the
        middle, right in front of me, is Now,
        and this is the only place any one of us
        have any control over.

What's coming along from the future is being passed along the conveyor belt.

It happens now and then it moves off into my past. I have to focus on the moment. I can't miss the moment.

Imagine I've got Lego bricks and I'm building a building here in front of me and all my attention is off up into the future to my left.

I can't see what I'm doing in the moment and this is when I start making mistakes and when I make mistakes here, they pass off down into my past on my right, as regrets.

What I find an awful lot of my clients are doing is they oscillate between their past and their future falling into an anxiety state because they're staring up ahead all of the time worrying about what's coming up.

And we don't know what's coming.

We have a pretty good idea about what's coming in the most part, but we have really no concrete evidence that any of that's going to happen.

Then we whizz down into our pasts and think, "Oh, I wish I hadn't done that. Oh, I should have done that better."

The reason that happens is because they weren't present, they weren't in the moment when they were doing what they were doing.

So I love this (conveyor belt) analogy. People that I work with find it very helpful to start seeing that actually, doing whatever it is you're doing in the moment, is the place you have the control over.

When you start doing this, what happens is you start to enjoy life more.

I'll give you a little example.

When my son was very small I lived in
India and we didn't have a bathtub so
I had a plastic bathtub for him, which
I would fill every night.

Obviously, I *had* to clean this bathtub
and usually I cleaned it with a "Oh,
god. I've got to cook dinner after this,
and I've just got to do this..."

I'd get all in the, *"I've got to do - I've got to
do things - that are coming in the future,"*
through to "Oh, and I *should* have
done that..."

Then this one day I decided that I was
going to clean this bathtub and I was
going to enjoy every moment of it.

I cleaned it with my full attention and
I deliberately loved every part of the
cleaning and the bathtub sparkled!

I probably cleaned it better than I had
ever cleaned anything before in my life
and I actually enjoyed the process
because I wasn't thinking about all the

things that were yet to come and I
wasn't dwelling on all the things that I
hadn't done.

I was just cleaning the bath a very
mundane, very ordinary thing to do.

That was probably 12 or 13 years ago
and I still remember cleaning that
bath, and it still reminds me of a time
when I really enjoyed living in that
moment.

The other thing that I say to people
that come in to see me is that I ask
them how they arrived at my office.

Usually they've driven in a car, so I say
"You've got two wing mirrors in your
car, but when you're driving where are
you looking?"

They all tell me the same thing, they're
all looking out of the windscreen and
that actually it would be foolish and
silly to be looking in the mirrors
constantly and trying to drive the car

forward when you're looking in the wing mirrors all the time.

The wing mirrors are really handy, it's a really good idea to peer into your future and see what's coming and it's a really good idea to just check in on the past and learn from mistakes or what went well.

It's a good thing to check in, but those aren't the places to live.

The place to *live* is right here, right now, in this moment.

Step 3. Who's Thoughts Are They Anyway?

Jon: So, step three?

Fiona: **Step three** is who's thoughts are they anyway?

We all rush around thinking that the thoughts that go through our heads belong to Us and are Ours.

In fact, we mistake that usually for thinking we *are our thoughts.*

When I explain to people that actually, you are not your thoughts, I usually get a bit of a blank stare because that's how we've related to ourselves all these years.

So if I was to ask you to hold out your

hand and I was to ask you "Who's hand is that?"

You would probably reply to me "Well, that's my hand."

And I would say "Yes, it is your hand."

Which would imply that you are something other than your hand. And that if I was to take your hand away in some way, you wouldn't disappear, you would still be you.

This is my body, this belongs to me. Which would imply that I am something other than this body?

This is my mind, which would imply that I am something other than my mind. These are my thoughts, which would imply that I am something other than my thoughts.

Therefore my thoughts *belong* to me.

When you start to really understand this principle it gives you control because now your thoughts belong to you and you can do whatever you want with them.

You can choose to act upon them or not. You can choose to believe them or not.

It puts the power of choosing how you react to the stimulus, to what happens to you in your life, squarely back in your court because you're the one that decides whether or not you want to believe these thoughts that are going on in your heads.

Our thoughts are very clever. I could ask you to think of a fluffy pink elephant and I'm sure in your mind you could create a fluffy pink elephant.

It doesn't make it a real thing, it doesn't make it something that actually exists, and a lot of our thoughts are like that.

We have thousands and thousands of thoughts every day and not all of them are true, not all of them are real.

In fact, most of them aren't. There's very, very few that are.

So understanding that your thoughts are yours, you can do what you like with them and you can choose which ones you act upon, gives you an immense amount of power in living your daily life, very happily.

Another thing that I find very interesting is this dialogue that goes on in our head.

It's a bit like the commentary box when you're watching sports and you've got the guys sitting there saying "And the ball's being passed to…" and they're commentating on what's happening in the game that you're watching.

But we all kind of have this

commentary box in our heads. We have this little voice that talks to us about stuff and again, this is my internal voice, it belongs to me. I can have control over what it says and what I believe of what it says.

So sometimes it's a really good idea to just turn the sound down and not listen to it.

Just don't bother listening to that chatter that goes on.

And the judgments that it tends to put forward, even if you listen to them, don't let them come out of your mouth.

I hear so many people just wandering about, making judgments about the people around them, making judgments about the weather and their lack of control. This commentary doesn't help you.

This doesn't help you to lead a happy

life, it just pulls you into this space of internal gossip and that is just a fictional thing, like an episode of a soap opera.

It's not real, it's just not real.

So who's thoughts are they anyway?

They're your thoughts and you have the control over what you do with those thoughts.

So deliberately take control of them and choose what you think.

Step 4. The Three P's

Jon: **Step four.**

Fiona: The three Ps.

The three Ps are:

- **Perception**

- **Perspective**

- **Personal belief**

I'll break those down a little bit for you. But first of all, I will just say to you that your mind and your body are not separate things they are part and parcel of the one organism and one effects the other in equal proportion.

So when something happens in your

mind your physiology will respond to whatever's going on in your mind.

The body doesn't need to know whether what's happening around is real or imagined, it will react in the same way.

We know that because if I say to you. . . imagine a lemon.

Imagine you have a lemon in your hand and just feel that lemon.

Just smell that lemon, a nice juicy lemon and it smells fresh and it smells of a sunny day.

I'd like you to imagine that if you were to cut that lemon into two and take both halves of that lemon and put it to your nose and take a deep, long breath of that fresh citrusy lemon smell.

You'll probably notice now that your mouth has started to salivate.

We know there was no lemon there at all but your body has started to respond to that. You'll know that when you smell food as you go past a restaurant you'll start to salivate.

So we know that you don't actually have to have the physical thing in front of you to have your body make a response to that.

So we're viewing our world through the three Ps.

We have our **Perceptions**, how we perceive the world around us.

We have our **Perspective**, which is where we're standing and looking at that world.

And we have what we **Personally** believe about that world.

The information that comes in through all of our senses gets passed through these three Ps.

I was around in the 1980s and I remember watching television. There was a fantastic advert for The Guardian newspaper.

This advert, which I'll describe to you, really sums up what I've been trying to explain there with the three Ps.

It was a black and white ad and it ran with an old man walking down the street and then the next shot was a skinhead youth running, and then you realised he was running at the old man.

All sorts of judgments, perceptions and perspectives came up in your mind.

Then the camera pulls way back and you see that there is a pile of bricks falling from above and it's going to hit the old man and actually this young guy is just running to grab the old man and pull him out of the way.

The caption used was "Get the full picture"

So the way we view our world is very much through these filters.

Perspective is a massive one.

We could be sitting in the same room and facing opposite directions.

I might be able to see a window and a cupboard and you might be able to see a bookshelf and a computer.

You and I would both go to a court of law and we would both swear that there was no window behind you, there was no bookshelf in the room I was in, and we'd both be right.

Our perspectives change the way we view the truth of what is actually happening.

People get very hung up on their beliefs of what happened and how it was. They stress and they worry and they get very confused about the reality of an issue.

Actually, what you need to do is you need to take whatever it is that's troubling you and almost pick it up like it's a physical thing and start to look at it from different ways.

Start to spin it around in your hand and look and ask yourself, "Is my belief true? Is my perception of this event actually real or did I miss something?"

When you realise that no matter how flat you make a pancake, there are always two sides to it. You'll find the effect that belief or that thought has on you, will change completely because you were only ever looking at it through your perceptions, from your perspective, and with your belief set.

Jon: Is there something very practical that we can do that actually helps us to do that, to change our perspective?

Fiona: Yes, separate yourself from the event and spend a quiet moment looking at it from different sides and appreciate that everything that happens will always be seen by the different people involved.

From their viewpoint, from their stance, and they might not have the information you have.

I don't have the information that you can see a bookshelf and you don't have the information that I can see a window. That is the fact of the matter and if I can just pick that up and say, "Ah, well maybe Jon could see a bookshelf."

Then I can understand what is actually happening an awful lot better and my responses, and my reactions, suddenly change.

Step 5. Catching Yourself At It!

Jon: And this is one of the ones I'm looking forward to. This is an intriguing title, step, stage or approach... **number five.**

Fiona: *Catching Yourself At It.*

This is about creating an awareness and starting to watch your thoughts.

We talked earlier about taking that thought and making it real in front of you and putting it outside of ourself and imagining it.

When you start to create this kind of awareness of your thoughts and you start to become conscious of your thinking, you can start to look at ways that your thinking creates tension, so there's "all the "I" tension".

When I say **I** tension people go "Eye tension?"

But **I** tension really is:
    I want,
    I wish,
    I am,
    I have…

All those **I** tensions that create that stress in your body.

So when you start becoming aware of the thoughts that you have that create that tension, then you can start doing something about it.

When I was doing my meditation courses in India, the first one I did, I got to probably the third or fourth day and I was desperately frustrated because calming this monkey mind was becoming a constant chore.

It just wouldn't calm down.

You get an opportunity, although it's a silent retreat, you do get an opportunity to speak to the teacher, so I took myself along and I said to him "Look, I just can't seem to control it. I've got these thoughts and they just keep coming into my head all the time and I can't do anything about them."

He very kindly looked at me and he said "Do people come to your home?" I said "Well, yes. Of course, they come to my home."
He said "So, what do you do when someone comes to your home? Do you let them in?"
"Oh, yes, yes. I let them in." I replied.
"And do you give them tea?"
"Yes."
"So you look after them?"
"Oh, yes, yes. I look after them." "Do you feed them?"
"Yes, normally I give them biscuits or something."

He said "So you really nurture them and look after them, and what do they do?"

"Well, they stay for a chat."
Then he said "And if you keep talking
to them, what do they do?"
So I said "Well, they stay."
He smiled and said "And your
thoughts are no different as visitors.
Your thoughts come to your mind and
you feed them, and let them in, and
nurture them, and look after them,
then they will stay. If you don't feed
them and look after them and nurture
them, what will they do?"

"Ah, they'll go away." I said quite
quietly.

This is a secret that is invaluable to
learn because this rumination, this
constant repetitive thought process
that we all entertain, it's a bit like the
news feed that we spoke of where they
just keep repeating the same news over
and over and over again.

This creates a huge amount of tension
in our minds and also in our bodies.
We often hold ourselves with that

tension and we get aches and we get pains and we get stressed and we get angry and we get tempers.

None of this helps to actually make our lives any easier at all.

So watch yourself, watch your thoughts, look at them and actually sit down and talk to them and say "Look, I'm really sorry. This isn't the time. I haven't got time to sit and spend time with you now. I will address you later. I will talk to you about, *whatever it is that's going on in your head,* I'll talk to you in three or four hours time when I've got a minute."

You'll find you get to three or four hours time and you won't even remember what it was that you were ruminating over earlier on in the day and you have avoided a whole heap of stress, and anxiety, and tension that was all needless.

Step 6. Dealing With Thomas

Jon: Brilliant - so let's move on to the next one?

Fiona: **The next one** is Dealing with Thomas.

We've all heard the phrase, '***Doubting Thomas***', so this section is really dedicated to doubt and how to deal with it.

When we feel doubt and we start questioning ourselves, we usually reach for something to make us feel safe and make us feel comfortable. This kind of leads me down two different avenues really. The first one is how we self-soothe.

A lot of people self-soothe with food, so they have eating disorders. Some people use drugs, some people use alcohol.

There are many other things that people use to self-soothe and none of this actually makes for a happy life because most people who overeat wish they didn't. Most people who drink too much wish they didn't.

Very few people are really happy with those habits that they've developed. Those habits are usually developed to self-soothe and that self-soothing comes in because they have doubting feelings.

The other thing we do when we doubt is we find someone else to blame.

We find someone else to shift the responsibility away from ourselves and give it to somebody else.

Very often it's the last person who actually needs to have that responsibility and it has nothing to do with them anyway. Because, as we've already discovered, these are our thoughts, these are our beliefs and they're within our control.

Let me tell you one of the things that I was told by a very old friend of mine who was a natural doctor.

He was an American guy and he said to me, "What you have to do is learn the 11th commandant and that is ***thou shalt not Should on thyself.***"

I think that's lovely. That "should" word.

I should have done this and I should have done that. Or you should have done this or you should have done that. That kind of sums up this whole doubting thing.

Again, if we can take hold of that thought and look at it and really examine where that is coming from. Is it true? Is it really true? Is what I'm believing about this situation right? And sometimes we have to go back to step one and just accept it for what it is.

There's a very good author, Stuart Wild, and he had a lovely quote, which was, "When in doubt, lean out."

I really like this quote because when you have that doubt, if you start pushing towards the things you have doubts about or pushing towards the things that aren't happening because you really want them to happen what you are doing is pushing away the good things and pushing towards things you don't want.

So when in doubt, lean out and just let it happen and go straight back to acceptance, watching and allowing whatever it is that needs to happen, to happen.

By taking the tension out of the situation, we can just allow, allowing it to happen.

Jon: How do we do that?

Fiona: How do we do that?

         Lean out.

         Mentally and physically lean away
         from the things that you're pushing
         towards. We spend a lot of time
         striving and trying to do things.

         I actually don't like the word trying at
         all because when you're trying you're
         putting a tension into the situation and
         when something's under tension it
         very rarely works effectively.

         We want to actually create a nice,
         relaxed environment.

         So breathing, allowing and just
         accepting the situation for how it is.

Jon: So taking a moment?

Fiona: Taking a moment, exactly. Just taking
         a moment.

Step 7. From Aargh to Ahhhh

Jon: So next chapter heading really intrigues me.

Fiona: Okay, the next chapter is from Aargh to Ahhhh (scream to sigh) and this involves a technique that I like to call '**No Thing Thinking**'.

This was actually summed up just recently by a friend of mine who said to me, "I have my best ideas when I'm not thinking."

Jon: That's also the concept behind Jamie Smart's book, 'Clarity' yes?

Fiona: Yes. We often find that we overthink things. It goes back to our rumination and the constant playing and playing and playing of ideas.

We often get stuck in a pattern of thinking where we can't find a solution because we get stuck in that rut if you like.

When you're driving on a road that's had the surface taken off and you find that you get pulled into the ruts that are lying beneath the road.

It's a little bit like that with our thinking.

What we need to do is find a space where we're *not* thinking.

Now we all have different ways of doing that, some people like to do gardening, some people like to go for a walk. Some people like to just be out in the country or play with their dog.

Jon: I spend time in the virtual reality world Second Life…

Fiona: There you are. There are many, many ways we can create a space in our lives where we are just not really thinking about anything and again, that puts us in this space of allowing.

Many years ago I did a course in India with an Indian teacher and he said it in a way that really made me giggle actually.

He said, "Why is it we always have our best ideas when we're in the bathroom?"

Well that's because actually, we have to be relaxed to use the bathroom, and we have to be relaxed to have our best ideas.

To allow that thinking to happen your mind has to be relaxed.

Allowing you to be able to stop, take yourself away from whatever it is that you're ruminating about and trying to find a solution for, and putting yourself in a space where you're very relaxed and you're actually having some fun, you're doing something you really like to do.

So maybe not the the bathroom... unless it's to bathe.

Painting, photography, we all have hobbies that we would do, "If only I had the time..."

Make the time, but it doesn't have to be a long time, it could be just a few moments, because it's in those moments that you have your best thinking and you have your best ideas when you're in that *No-Thing Thinking* stage.

And then you can go from frustration and from Aargh to Ahhhh, there's the answer.

Step 8. Getting Latitude With Gratitude

Jon: And the next part of the daily application of Emotion Lotion is?

Fiona: **The next idea** is *Getting Latitude With Gratitude.*

Gratitude is possibly one of the most powerful things we can adopt in our lives.

We live fantastic lives, even when we don't think we do.

There are always good aspects of our lives happening. The trouble is with the way that most people think when they have mental hygiene issues is they tend to focus on what's not working for them.

They tend to focus on the things that they perceive as negative or bad.

Going back to Carl Jung, what we resist, persists. What we focus on, reveals itself.

When you adopt gratitude into your life and start using gratitude, what we actually find, and they've done a lot of studies on this now, is that the neural pathways in our brain, actually change.

Neural pathways are a little bit like any other pathway really and I like to explain this way...

You have your rubbish bin out of your back door at the end of the garden. You walk every day with your rubbish down to put it in the bin, and doing so you will create a nice, strong pathway down to your bin.

The grass will stop growing and you'll get a nice, really clear earth path and you'll be able to find this path whether it's dark or light, it doesn't matter.

You can just step out of your back door and you know where to go because that path has been created and it's a strong path.

If we were to then take that bin and move it to somewhere else in the garden now when you come out of the back door you start walking towards the bin and what's going to happen?

We're going to create a brand new path, which will become stronger the more we use it and this old path will just grow over and disappear.

So if we apply this to the way we think about things, if we're having a constant negative thought or a negative belief, what we find is that we can actually rush down that path really easily because it's one we thought many, many, many times before.

But if we actually start to think in

different ways and start to be grateful for the things in our lives, we find that we move that target and new pathways are created and we start to see our lives in very different ways.

A very simple thing that you can do is go and buy yourself a nice notebook.

Keep it next to the bed and every night write down five things to be grateful for that day.

This sounds very simple. And I have clients sometimes sit in front of me and they can't even think of one thing to be grateful for and this I find quite incredible that people are going through their lives really not able to see the good in their lives.

Jon: The problem is?

Fiona: The problem is you're only looking for the big thing… but these things to be grateful for can be anything.

They can be "I'm grateful for my eyes because I can see". They can be "I'm grateful for somebody who let me in, in the traffic, today". They can be:

- "I'm grateful for my health."

- "I'm grateful for my family."

- "I'm grateful for the roof over my head."

- "I'm grateful for the food on the table."

- "I'm grateful for the child that smiled at me this morning."

There are so many things and when you start looking at what's good in your life you start seeing more things that are good in your life and more happiness comes because you start to realise that actually, your life ain't so bad.

There's always somebody worse off

than you are and if you're grateful for what you have in your life this empowers you in a way that has, I think, miraculous effects upon the way you start seeing the world around you and I can't emphasise this enough.

This one thing alone will change your life and change your levels of happiness beyond anything that I could possibly mention!

So if there's one part of this you take on, make that Gratitude.

But write it down.

It's good to think it, it's good to go, "Oh, I'm really grateful for this and I'm grateful for that" but actually writing it down gives it substance, it gives it reality. And it also gives you something to go back over and look at and realise how good your life actually is.

Jon: There is a lot of studies on this isn't there?

Fiona: Yes... You can actually go online and you can find lots of apps and things that use gratitude but typing it in doesn't have the same effect.

Thinking it doesn't have the same effect...

The neurology of actual muscle memory behind your personal handwriting and seeing your hand when you read it back just has a different effect.

Write it and you move those bins much, much more quickly and find suddenly that life really is good.

Step 9. Rubber boundaries

Jon: Brilliant, so tell me about the next strategy and why does it bounce?

Fiona: These are Rubber Boundaries.

Boundaries are really important parts of our lives and we often neglect to set them up.

If I wind back a little bit, we all operate at our best when we operate from a place of security and comfort.

So when we operate from within our comfort zone, what this allows us to do is push our boundaries from the inside.

If we try and drag our boundaries, our comfort zone, if you like, from the outside, we found we end up with a very spiky kind of shape.

[*Publishers note: To demonstrate this Fiona holds a rubber band on her finger tips...*]

Fiona: When we operate from within our Rubber Boundaries, we're safe and we're comfortable and we know what we're doing.

That doesn't mean we can't grow because a Rubber Boundary can stretch.

A Rubber Boundary can become a lot bigger.

But if we try and stretch that rubber boundary from the outside, we get a very particular shaped, quite angular, uncomfortable space. It takes us out of being secure and feeling safe.

But when we *push* our boundaries, and we've all used that phrase with our children, you know, "Just pushing your boundaries" that's exactly when you want a push from the inside.

You don't want to try and drag from the outside.

Boundaries are really important to work from, from a place of safety and from a place of comfort and they're really important to set up not just for yourself but for the people around you.

If we don't set up clear boundaries, what we find is people cross those boundaries and then we find ourselves compromised and doing things we don't want to be doing.

We've all said yes to things we didn't want to do.

If we have clear boundaries, people don't even bother to cross over that line because they're apparent, people can see them.

If you think of somebody that you really respect, somebody in your life that you look at and you think, "That person is somebody I really hold in high esteem." The one thing that is probably going to be true about that person, is that you *know* exactly where you stand with them.

There are no grey areas and that is because they will have set up very clear boundaries.

When you set up those clear boundaries for yourself, it allows you to live your life knowing that nobody is going to cross them.

Nobody is going to start telling you what to do and how to be and how to live your life. You'll be operating from inside your safety space and you'll be able to grow and stretch at a rate that's comfortable for you and nobody will come and disturb you, and this is incredibly powerful.

This was actually, something that came to me many years ago.

I was in Niagara and I was in one of those shops that sells the cups and the t-shirts and all that sort of stuff.

I kept on seeing all these key rings and things with WWJD written on them. I just thought it was the local radio station or something.

I kept on looking and it was everywhere in this shop and then one of them I actually turned over and it said, "What would Jesus do?"

I thought what a fantastic way of allowing people from that belief system to think when they're not sure how to behave or what to do or how to act, to just sit there and think of the one person that they completely trust and believe in and say, "Well, what *would* Jesus do in this position?"

I've kind of adapted that a little bit and I've made that any sort of hero, your hero.

That could be your grandad.

It could be a fictional character.

It could be your spiritual leader.

It could be anybody but it has to be somebody that you really look up to.

Then, when you don't know what to do, you just stop and think, "What would grandad do?", "What would the Dalai Lama do?", "What would Jesus do?"

Use whoever works for you and you will find that by putting yourself in their shoes you will make a far better decision for yourself and your end result will be safe, secure and within your comfort zone.

Step 10. Apply Daily!

Jon: And, finally?

Fiona: **Finally, is Emotion Lotion** and
          applying that *Daily*.

          Emotion Lotion is the gathering
          together of all of these things and
          applying them into your life, every
          day.

          This might appear to be quite a lot to
          change, but actually if we look at the
          habits you've got yourself into, the
          habits of poor mental hygiene.

          The habits of possibly overeating or
          drinking a little too much wine of an
          evening, these are habits that you've
          managed to create quite easily, and
          this is as easy to get in place.

Habits are easy to create and if you can create a habit around doing the mirror exercise first thing in the morning, "I love you for who you are and who you are not."

Taking time to breathe, noticing your breath, putting yourself in the moment.

It's quite good to notice the beginning of your breath, the little space at the beginning and the little space at the end of your breath, that's the beginning of the next breath.

If you can start noticing those spaces, you'll become completely entrenched in that one moment.

If you start watching your thoughts, start taking those beliefs and those thoughts and putting them outside of yourself and looking at them and turning them round and seeing them from different perspectives.

Looking at your thoughts and reactions and saying, "Well, is that true? Is it real?"

Looking at them with curiosity and interest, "Oh, that's interesting."

If somebody says something to you, don't react, just go, "Oh, that was interesting." Look at how it made you feel... Well, that *was* interesting."

Not actually proportioning any positive or negative to it. It just was.

Looking at your thoughts as guests and how much you're actually entertaining these negative thoughts. How much time are you giving to these thoughts that are bringing you nothing?

Then when in doubt, lean out.

This becomes a phrase to live by.

"When in doubt, lean out".

And find a space every single day that you can just relax. Do something you enjoy doing.

Read the book, paint the painting, take the photograph, walk the dog.

Whatever it is that gives you that space to just switch those thoughts off.

Gratitude, again I can't express how important this is.

Start writing those five things every day without fail before you go to bed.

What this does is you actually go to bed thinking of five really nice things that happened in the day instead of going to bed thinking, "Oh, god I've got to get up in the morning. Oh, I've got... I've got, the bosses. I've got a presentation. I've got to do this," whatever it is that you're thinking.

Have that boundary discipline.

Set up those boundaries.

Start looking at where you've placed your boundaries and how much you need to stretch from your place of comfort, to allow yourself to have really healthy boundaries placed around who you really are.

This is something you can apply every single day and if you do this your happiness, your peace, your calm, your quality of sleep will get better and will improve.

Mistakes, Myths and Misunderstandings to Avoid

Jon: Okay. Fiona, mistakes, myths, and misunderstandings for our solopreneur audience to avoid.

#1 Mistake: Thinking you're out of control

Jon: What is, in your opinion and your experience, the number one mistake you see people making?

Fiona: People thinking that they're out of control or that they have no control over their thoughts.

This is clearly not the case.

The amount of control you have is all

down to understanding that your
thoughts are not you and that they're
yours to do what you want to with.

#1 Myth: You're 'likely' to become mentally ill

Jon: And for somebody who's spent so
long in meditation in India and
working with holy men, what's the
biggest myth that you see perpetuated
towards people who are self-
employed, solopreneur, people who
are in the business?

Fiona: Crisis happens to everyone.

We can't stop life happening and stuff
happens in life that isn't nice. When
that happens people feel out of
control. They often worry terribly that
they will become mentally ill.

I think with all the attention that's
being placed on 'mental illness' at the
moment, its negative side is that it is

creating a fear of our mental equilibrium, our mental state.

80% of people will never go anywhere near being mentally ill and, of the 20% that do, an awful lot of them it will be a very temporary thing no worse than a cold or flu.

So this fear of being mentally ill and not being able to manage life, I think, is yes, a bit of a myth.

#1 Misunderstanding: Mental medication is the answer

Jon: And a misunderstanding, something that people just aren't getting right?

Fiona: Again, it's when people find themselves under pressure.

People find themselves in a situation they've never had to deal with before and they get that tension and they get the stress to go with it.

Feeling stressed and out of sorts they think they have to go and get medicated and that medication is the only answer available to them, and it's not.

No medication comes without its own price.

And actually, if you can sort this yourself by sorting out the way you think and the way you perceive the world around you, you'll find you can get through this very easily without having to take medications.

Massive Motivation

Jon: Thank you. Now tell us more about
the benefits of applying Emotion
Lotion daily?

Get A Better Work-Life Balance

Fiona: One of the benefits is your work-life
balance, and this is a phrase we hear an
awful lot of.

When you're a solopreneur, an
entrepreneur or any sort of business
owner, it's a very blurred line between
when you're working and when you're
at home.

We probably work more hours as a
solopreneur than we would if we
actually had a proper job.

So this balance can become quite a blur for us.

By applying your Emotion Lotion every day, what happens is you start enjoying your life so much more, then that blur just doesn't matter because you're enjoying every part of your life.

You're enjoying every moment in your life.

So whatever it is that you're doing, whether it's working, or maybe you're at home with your family or you're down at the gym, whatever it is that you like to do, you're in the moment and you're enjoying that moment.

Therefore, it doesn't matter whether you're 'working' or you're off or whatever you're doing, you're having a good time.

Enjoy More Time

Jon: And you're going to enjoy more of that time?

Fiona: We're going to enjoy a lot more of that time, because by being in the moment, time becomes stretchy.

You actually enjoy more time by living in the moment and enjoying time more.

More time for being grateful for what you have.

More time for applying your Emotion Lotion every day.

Instead of living in the past and in the future, you're living now and now lasts forever.

There is no time in now.

Live Every Day of Your Life

Jon: What do you mean by live every day of your life?

Fiona: I mean really taking the bull by the horns and doing what you want to do.

Really making choices that support you.

Living life as your true authentic self, on your terms and enjoying it, having fun.

We were all put on this beautiful planet and you know what? It's actually a big playground for us to play in and enjoy every single day and the joy is found, in the moment.

Jon: Fiona Ross, this has been really, really enjoyable. Thank you so much.

Fiona: Thank you very much.

Jon: And of course as with all HypnoArts

Author Experts work, if you're reading this as a book first, it will also be available as an audio book, a video tutorial with a bonus questions and answers section, and even as a group or page on FaceBook.

Just search for Emotion Lotion Apply Daily!

Use hashtag
#EmotionLotionApplyDaily

To get all details and to contact Fiona for appearances and speaking events go to EmotionLotion.co.uk

Or connect directly with her agent at HypnoArts.com

Meet Fiona Ross

Photograph by Ingrid Weel

After achieving my early career goals becoming a Training Manager and Educator for some of the UK's top hair and beauty companies, I began an 18-year personal search for meaning that would change the course of my life. It took me across many continents and provided many wonderful opportunities and insights.

My work as a consultant gave me the opportunity to conduct training seminars, shows and workshops for hundreds of people across India and South East Asia.

Returning to the UK, I consolidated my experience, knowledge and insight with qualifications in:

Advanced Hypnosis and Subconscious Mind Coaching.

Educational Performance

Neuro Linguistic Programming (Master Practitioner)

Motivational Coaching

Emotional Freedom Technique (EFT)

Stress Management

Postword
by: Jonathan Chase

Unlike a foreword I prefer to put my comments after the fact simply because then we're partially sure you've read, heard or otherwise digested this work.

I am really grateful that I get to assist wonderfully attentive people like Fiona to get their work out into the world.

And into your hands.

I've no doubt that you've tried to do the right thing to maintain your mental hygiene and remain sane.

I know I have but it has always seemed to be so time consuming.

But, even as we were filming this interview, some of the approaches Fiona has fine tuned and perfected were begging to happen with little or no effort. And I like easy.

Unlike a foreword I'm not here to tell you to read the book; I'm here to tell you to read it again, and again.

As with all #HypnoArtsBooks you should be able to do that on an average commute into town, definitely while you're waiting for your cancelled flight, or over a couple of lunches.

Our authors don't do fluff or fancy passages full of rhetoric, we don't do the 'bigger the book the better the content' thing.

So go back and read it again. Make notes in the margins.

Fold page corners to mark the best bits.

Spill coffee and tea on the cover...

READ the book and allow it to help your life change.

Enhance Your Lifestyle Experience. Now.

HypnoArts Publications
Enhancing the Experience of Life

For the most up to date information on;
Books, Audio, Courses and Video Tutorials,
Author information, links to forums
and FaceBook groups Live Author Appearances and events
download the free #HypnoArts App
from iTunes App Store or Google Play

or Visit **HypnoArts.com**
and grab your copy of our email newsletter.

We look forward to meeting you.
Jane Bregazzi. CEO HypnoArts

Notes:

Lightning Source UK Ltd.
Milton Keynes UK
UKOW01f2026290917
310140UK00005B/290/P